First publ
Gill and M
Gold
Du
with associat
London, New Yo
Johannesburg, Lagos, Melbourne,
Singapore, Tokyo

Design and artwork by Della Varilly and Patricia McElroy

Cover design by Frank Spiers/Della Varilly

Typesetting by Cahill and Co., East Wall Road, Dublin

7171 1208 X

New Words

Page 3
pleased
sun
shining
stronger

Page 4
about
wearing
coat
warm

Page 5
began
around
more
How
today

Page 6
any
if
just
smiled

Page 7
shone
over
stopped

Page 8
under

Page 10
table
card
Ruth
hospital
Sam
soon

Page 11
hope
doctor
stay
lift
floor

Page 12
orange
book
know

Page 13
friend
leg
plaster

Page 15
broken
hurt
cried

Page 16
nurse
work
roller skates
should

Page 18
everyone
something
time

Page 20
Snow
during
night
everything
white

Page 21
great
our
yet

Page 22
school
snowman
slowly
must

Page 24
wait
boys
snowball

Page 26
before
carrot
nose
old
scarf

Page 27
dinner

Page 28
mice
outside
mouse
hole
fat
watching

Page 30
only
noise
sing
bird
or

Page 31
meeting
tonight
think
others
tell

Page 35
why

Page 36
stood
bell
neck

Page 37
Listen

Page 39
afraid

Page 40
still
nothing
easy

Page 42
garden
best
swing

Page 43
bushes
nest
twigs
moss

Page 44
yellow
beak
feathers

Page 45
food
lays
eggs

Page 46
Every
near
mother
father

Page 47
Quickly
shouted
help
lucky

Page 48
inside

Page 49
trying
fly
branches

Page 53
Peter
gate

Page 54
swim
pond
quacked
talked

Page 57
happened

Page 58
long
fast
gobbled

Page 60
rope
snapped

Page 61
caught
tail
tied
end

Page 62
zoo

Page 63
pull

The Sun and the Wind

The wind had been blowing all morning. He was very pleased with himself. He looked up at the sun shining over the hills and fields.

'I'm stronger than you,' said the wind to the sun.

'No, you are not,' said the sun.

'Yes, I am!' said the wind.

---

pleased sun shining stronger

'Very well then,' said the sun. 'We'll see about that. Do you see that man over there?'

'Yes, I do,' said the wind. 'He is wearing a big coat.'

'Let's see who can make him take off his big warm coat,' said the sun.

'I'll go first,' said the wind. 'I will make him take off that big warm coat.'

---

about   wearing   coat   warm

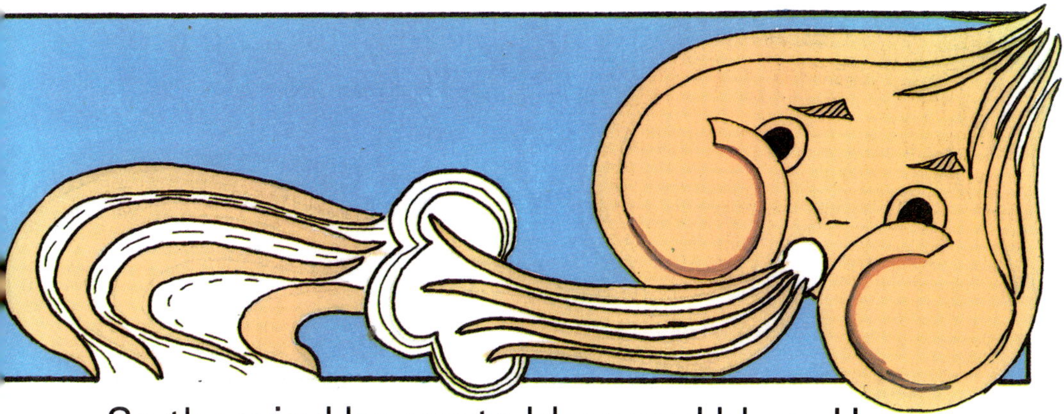

So the wind began to blow and blow. He blew all around the man. He blew the trees and the flowers. He blew the man and his big warm coat.

But the more the wind blew, the more the man loved his big coat. He would not let it blow away.

'How strong the wind is today!' said the man. 'I'm so happy to have this lovely warm coat.'

began around more how today

The wind blew and blew all around the man. Then he said, 'I cannot blow any more. No one can make that man take off his big warm coat. If I cannot do it, no one can. No one is as strong as I am.'

But the sun just smiled at the wind. 'I will shine now,' he said, 'and we will see.'

any if just smiled

So the sun began to shine. He shone all over the man and his big warm coat. The man began to get a little warm. And then he got very, very hot!

'The wind has stopped now,' said the man. 'And the sun is shining. Now it's too hot for this big coat.'

---

shone over stopped

So the man took off his coat and sat down under a tree where it was not so hot.

'You see,' said the sun, smiling. 'You blew and blew and blew. But you could not make the man take off his big coat. I shone all around him and he took it off. So I am stronger than you are.'

'Yes,' said the wind. 'So you are.'

under

Waiters

Dining with his older daughter,
Dad forgot to order water.
Daughter quickly called the waiter.
Waiter said he'd bring it later.

So she waited, did the daughter,
Till the waiter brought the water.
When he poured it for her later,
Which one would you call the waiter?

Mary Ann Hoberman

A Gift for Ruth

Kate was sitting at the table when her Mammy came in.

'What are you doing, Kate?' she asked.

'I'm making a card for Ruth,' said Kate. 'I want to take it when I go to see her in hospital. I have a gift for her, but I wanted to make a card to go with it.'

'Ruth will like the gift you got for her,' said Mammy. 'And she will like getting a card too. Could I see it?'

'There,' said Kate. 'That's it. Do you like it, Mammy?'

'It's just lovely, Kate,' said Mammy. 'Now you had better go and get your coat and hat. Sam and his Mammy will be here soon to take you to the hospital.'

---

table card Ruth hospital Sam soon

'I hope Ruth will be a bit better today,' said Sam when they went into the hospital.

'I hope so too,' said his Mammy. 'The doctor said she would have to stay for a day or so after she fell. But I hope she will be coming home soon.'

'So do I,' said Kate.

'Let's get into the lift now,' said Sam's Mammy. 'We have to go up to the third floor to see Ruth.'

hope doctor stay lift floor

'What have you got in that bag, Sam?' Kate asked when they got out of the lift.

'I have some apples and a bottle of orange for Ruth,' he said.

'I see you have a bag too, Kate,' said Sam's Mammy.

'Yes,' said Kate. 'I have a gift for Ruth. Mammy and I got her a book at the shop. And I made a card for her this morning. I hope she will like them.'

'I know she will,' said Sam's Mammy. 'It was very good of you to get a gift for Ruth.'

'A book is a good thing when you have to stay in bed all day,' said Sam.

---

orange book know

'There's Ruth now,' said Kate when she saw her friend. 'And she has her leg in a plaster!'

'Mammy!' said Ruth. 'I'm so happy to see you. I have been sitting here just hoping that you would come. I hoped Sam and Kate would come too. And here they are!'

'How is your leg today?' Kate asked her friend.

'It's a bit better,' said Ruth. 'But the doctor says I have to stay here for a day or so.'

friend leg plaster

'We came up in the lift to the third floor,' said Sam. 'And look what we have for you.'

Sam took the apples and the bottle of orange out of the bag. Then Ruth opened Kate's gift.

'What a lovely book,' said Ruth. 'I have not seen this one. Thank you, Kate. And thank you for the card too. You are a good friend.'

'How would you all like an apple?' asked Sam and Ruth's Mammy.

'This is just lovely,' said Sam. 'I would like to come and stay in hospital too.'

'You would not think it was so lovely if you had broken your leg,' said their Mammy. 'Ruth was not at all happy just after she fell.'

'No, I was not,' said Ruth. 'My leg hurt and I cried and cried.'

'Yes, I know you did,' said Sam. 'It was a good thing that Mammy had the car at home that day.'

---

broken think hurt cried

'Did you cry when the doctor put the plaster on your leg?' asked Kate. 'Did it hurt?'

'Just a little,' said Ruth. 'But the doctor and the nurse were very good to me so it was not so bad. They let Mammy stay with me for a little bit. Then Daddy came to see me when he got home from work.'

'Did the doctor say that you could not play with your roller skates again?' asked Sam.

'He said I could skate again when my leg was better,' said Ruth. 'But he said that I should not have been speeding down the street like that.'

---

nurse work roller skates should

'Did you not see the bit of rock?' asked Kate.

'No,' said Ruth. 'I was having fun speeding down the hill on my roller skates and I did not see it at all.'

'Does your leg hurt in that plaster?' asked Sam.

'Just a little,' said Ruth.

'The plaster is very hard,' said Sam.

'Yes, it is,' said Kate.

'Good morning, everyone,' said the nurse as she came in. 'How are you all today? The girls are going to have something to eat now,' said the nurse. 'So it's time for everyone to go home. Your friends can come and see you again after you eat.'

'Thank you all for coming to see me,' said Ruth. 'And thanks again for all the lovely things.'

everyone something time

A Blink

A blink I think, is the same as a wink,
A blink is a wink that grew,
For a *wink* you wink with only one eye,
And a *blink* you blink with two!

Jacqueline Segal

Snow

Snow fell softly during the night. Kate was sleeping in her lovely warm bed and she did not see it. In the morning when she looked out, everything was white.

The houses and the streets were white and so were the trees and paths. Their car was all white with snow too.

Snow during night everything white

'Mammy, did you see all that lovely white snow?' asked Kate. 'It has fallen all over the houses and the streets. And our car is all white too. Everything looks just great!'

'Yes,' said Mammy. 'The snow looks lovely but it is a very cold morning. Eat up now and we will be on our way. Is Mark up yet?'

'I did not hear him,' said Kate, 'But I can go and have a look.'

'You eat up your porridge, Kate,' said Mammy. 'I'll go and see if Mark is up.'

great our yet

'Did you see all that snow?' asked Mark as he came in and sat down at the table. 'We will have great fun playing in the snow after school today.'

'Yes,' said Kate. 'We could make a snowman.'

'Where is Daddy?' asked Mark.

'He is on his way to work with Sam's daddy,' said Mammy. 'It will take them some time to get to work this morning. The cars will have to go very slowly.'

'Did you see the snow falling during the night?' asked Mark.

'No,' said Mammy. 'I was asleep in my warm bed and I did not see a thing. Eat up now. We must be on our way very soon.'

---

school snowman slowly must

'Put on your warm coats and hats,' said Mammy when they had eaten. 'I'll take you to school in the car today.'

'Could we walk to school this morning?' asked Mark.

'It's too cold to walk this morning,' said Mammy. 'You can walk home after school if it is not snowing too hard.'

'Then we can go out and make that snowman, Kate,' said Mark.

Mark and Kate put on their warm coats and hats and off they went to school in the car.

Kate and Mark and their friends could not wait for school to be over. They loved school, but it was hard to work with all that lovely snow around.

Mark wanted to play with the boys. He wanted to make snowballs and have fun.

Kate hoped the lovely white snow would fall again. She wanted to walk in the soft white snow and make a snowman with her friends.

wait boys snowball

Kate was walking home with her friend Ruth when a soft wet snowball hit her coat. Soon everyone was making snowballs and getting very wet. But they were all having a very good time.

'I'm getting a bit cold,' Kate said to Ruth. 'Let's go home and get something warm to eat. Then we can go out and make a snowman.'

'What lovely hot tea this is,' said Mark. 'Thank you, Mammy. I was getting a bit cold and wet.'

'Are you warm again, Mark?' asked Kate. 'Ruth and I want to go out and make a snowman before Daddy comes home from work.'

Mammy gave them a funny black hat to put on the snowman. And she gave them a carrot for his nose. Ruth helped Kate and Mark make the snowman and he got bigger and bigger.

'Daddy has an old scarf he does not want,' said Ruth. 'I will run home and get it.'

---

before   carrot   nose   old   scarf

When Ruth came back with the old scarf, they put it on the snowman.

'Our snowman looks great,' said Kate.

'I love his funny carrot nose,' said Ruth.

'Here comes Daddy now,' said Kate. 'He is just in time to see the snowman.'

'He looks just great,' said Daddy. 'I loved making snowmen when I was a boy.'

'Time to come in now,' called Mammy. 'Your dinner is on the table. It will be as cold as that snowman if you don't come in soon!'

'Good-bye everyone,' said Ruth. 'I will see you in the morning, Kate and Mark.'

Daddy smiled. 'And you will see our friend the snowman too,' he said.

---

dinner

A Bell for the Cat

All the little mice lived under the floor in a big white house. Outside a fat cat sat waiting and watching.

'Look at that fat cat,' said a baby mouse as he looked out of the hole. 'He sits there all day, just waiting and watching. What is he waiting for?' he asked.

'He is waiting for one of us,' said his Mammy.

'Does he want to play with us?' asked the baby mouse.

'What a funny little mouse you are!' cried all the mice. 'That cat does not want to play with us. He wants to eat us!'

'That cat walks so softly,' said one little mouse. 'We cannot hear him when he comes.'

'And we cannot hear him when he goes away!' said a second mouse. 'If that cat sits there all day, we cannot go out and look for things to eat.'

---

mice outside mouse hole fat watching

‘If only he would make a noise,’ said a little mouse. ‘Then we would know when he was there.’

‘If only he would sing like a bird.’

‘If only he would huff and puff like a wolf.’

‘But cats do not sing like birds,’ said a big mouse. ‘And they do not huff and puff or make noise. They just walk very, very softly. And that is very, very bad for little mice like us!’

‘We will have to do something about that cat,’ they all said.

---

only   noise   sing   bird   or

'I know what we could do,' said a big brown mouse. 'We could call a meeting. We could ask all the mice we know to come to a meeting tonight. Then we could all think of something to do.'

'Good,' said all the others. 'We will ask the field mice and the house mice to come to our meeting. Then we can think of something to do.'

'A meeting! A meeting!' cried all the little mice. 'This is going to be fun! Let's go now and tell all our friends!'

'Not yet,' said the big brown mouse. 'Look outside and tell me what you see.'

meeting tonight others tell

When they looked out, there was the fat cat, sitting and watching and waiting.

'He's asleep,' said the baby mouse.

'You cannot tell when a cat is asleep,' said his Mammy. 'He could have one eye open, just waiting for one of us to come out. We will have to wait. And when the little girl calls him for dinner, one of us can go and tell our friends to come to the meeting tonight.'

So they waited and waited. And when the little girl called the cat, the big brown mouse said, 'I will go now and tell everyone to come to our meeting.'

And off he went to tell their friends.

First he told all the house mice.

'We'll be there,' they said. 'We just have to do something about that cat.'

Then he went to see his friends the field mice.

'We'll be there too,' they all said.

Night came, and the fat cat went up to sleep on the little girl's lovely warm bed. Then, one by one, all the mice began to come in. Field mice and house mice, big mice and little mice—all of them came to the meeting.

When everyone was there the big brown mouse said, 'Thank you all for coming to this meeting. You all know that something has to be done about that cat. He walks very softly and we cannot hear him come or go.'

'We know all about that cat,' said the old field mouse. 'He comes into our field and jumps on any mouse he can see. We cannot hear him come and we cannot hear him go.'

'That is why we called this meeting,' said the big brown mouse. 'Who can think of something to do?'

---

why

At first, no one could think of a thing. They all sat, thinking and thinking. Then a middle-sized house mouse stood up.

'I know what we should do,' he said.

'You do?' cried the others. 'Tell us!'

'We should get a bell for the cat,' said the middle-sized house mouse. 'We could put it around the cat's neck. Then he would make a noise as he walks and we could tell when he was coming or going. Any bell would do. It could be any bell at all!'

'Good!' cried all the other mice. 'That's just what we'll do!' And away they all went to look for a bell.

stood bell neck

They ran softly up and down. Over chairs and under beds, into presses and under beds, all looking for a bell for the cat.

'Here's something,' said one little mouse. 'Listen. Can you hear it? It makes a little noise.'

'A bell!' said his friend. 'A bell for the cat! It's just what we have been looking for! Let's go tell everyone!'

Listen

Back in the hole, all the mice were very happy.

'We have a bell,' they all said. 'We have a bell for the cat! Let's wait and listen to the big brown mouse. He will tell us what to do now.'

'Good work, everyone,' said the big brown mouse as he stood up. 'You all looked very hard and now we have a bell for the cat.'

Then they all looked at the mouse who said they should get a bell for the cat.

'Here you are, mouse,' said the big brown mouse. 'Off you go to put the bell on the cat.'

Everyone looked at the middle-sized house mouse. Everyone waited to hear what he would say.

'I know I said we should get a bell,' he said. 'But now I think one of you should go and put it on the cat.'

He looked at the big brown mouse and said, 'You are a very big mouse. You could do it.'

But the big brown mouse said, 'I cannot go. I must stay here and look after everyone. So I cannot go.'

'And I cannot go,' said the baby mouse. 'I am too little.'

'And I cannot go,' said his Mammy. 'I must stay and look after my little ones.'

'We cannot go,' said all the field mice. 'We are too afraid. We live in our lovely green fields and we are afraid to run around in this big house.'

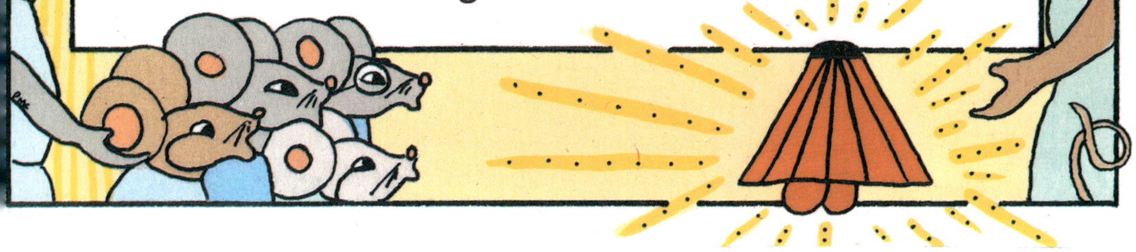

afraid

Then the oldest field mouse stood up. All the mice sat very still and waited to hear what he had to say.

'There is nothing we can do,' he said. 'It was very easy for us to think of something to do. But now we know that it is not so easy to do it.'

'There is nothing we can do,' they all said sadly. 'We have this lovely bell for the cat, but there is nothing we can do.'

So back to their homes they all went.

Today, you would see them all,
waiting and watching and sitting
very, very still as they listen
for the cat.

still nothing easy

Mice

I think mice
Are rather nice.
Their tails are long,
Their faces small,
They haven't any
Chins at all.
Their ears are pink,
Their teeth are white,
They run about
The house at night.
They nibble things
They shouldn't touch
And no one seems
To like them much.
But I think mice
Are nice.

Rose Fyleman

The Garden

Ruth had a lovely big garden at the back of her house. There were flowers and trees in the garden, but best of all there was a great big swing. Ruth's Daddy had made the swing.

If you got one good push when you were on the swing, you could look over the walls at the other gardens.

Kate loved to come to Ruth's garden and play with her on the great big swing.

---

garden best swing

One day when Kate was getting off the swing, she saw a small black thing in the bushes. 'Is that a ball?' she said to herself. 'I must go and have a look.'

So off she hopped and ran over to the bushes. And there she saw a bird's nest made of twigs and moss.

'That nest looks lovely and warm,' Kate said to herself. 'Ruth!' she called. 'I can see a little bird's nest here in the bushes. Some birds have made a nest of twigs and moss.'

'We must watch for the birds who are building this nest,' said Ruth. 'We must stay back a little so the birds are not afraid. Let's go sit by that tree and stay very still.'

---

bushes nest twigs moss

As Kate and Ruth were sitting by the tree, they saw a bird hop onto the bushes. They stayed very still and waited to see if he would go into the nest.

'What a lovely little bird,' said Ruth. 'He has a very yellow beak and his feathers are as black as can be.'

'He is a blackbird,' said Kate. 'Now we know that a blackbird is building that nest.'

---

yellow beak feathers

Into the nest hopped the little blackbird. Kate and Ruth sat very still and they watched and waited as he flew away again.

'This must be our secret,' Kate said to Ruth. 'We must not tell the boys. We will look after the blackbirds and we will leave some food for them.'

Ruth said, 'We will watch and see if the Mammy bird lays some eggs in the nest. Then we can watch the baby birds too.'

'This is going to be great fun,' said Kate.

---

food lays eggs

Every day, Kate and Ruth went to look at the nest. They looked and looked, but they did not go too near the nest. And one day, Ruth saw three lovely eggs in the nest.

'Look,' said Ruth. 'Can you see into the nest, Kate? The mother bird is there now and she is sitting on three little eggs.'

'Yes, I can see her,' said Kate. 'Her beak is not yellow and her feathers are brown, not black.'

'Here comes the father bird now,' said Ruth. 'He must be looking after the mother and the little eggs,'

Every near mother father

One day, Kate and Ruth came running into the garden after school. They wante to see if the baby birds were there yet. As they got there, they saw the cat looking at something in the bushes.

'Quickly!' shouted Kate. 'Get that cat! He is looking at something in the bushes!'

The cat ran away as Ruth came running down the garden. 'You bad cat!' she shouted.

'I know what he was looking at,' said Kate. 'Look. A baby bird has fallen out of the nest. Come and help me put him back.'

The girls took the soft little baby and put him back into the nest.

'You are a very lucky little bird,' they said.

Quickly shouted help lucky

Every day after that, when Kate and Ruth went to look at the nest, they could see three little babies inside.

When the mother bird came with food, they all opened their little beaks.

'They eat so much food,' said Kate.

'Look,' said Ruth. 'The father bird is helping too. He is coming with more food for the babies.'

---

inside

'I think the little birds are trying to fly,' Ruth said one day. The girls were watching the baby birds sit on the branches and fly from one to the other.

'They are not so little now,' said Kate. 'They are getting bigger and bigger. Soon they will all fly away.'

'I hope they will come back again when they are big,' said Ruth. 'They could come back to build nests of their own. If they do, we could tell the others about our secret.'

'Yes,' said Kate. 'I think we could.'

---

trying fly branches

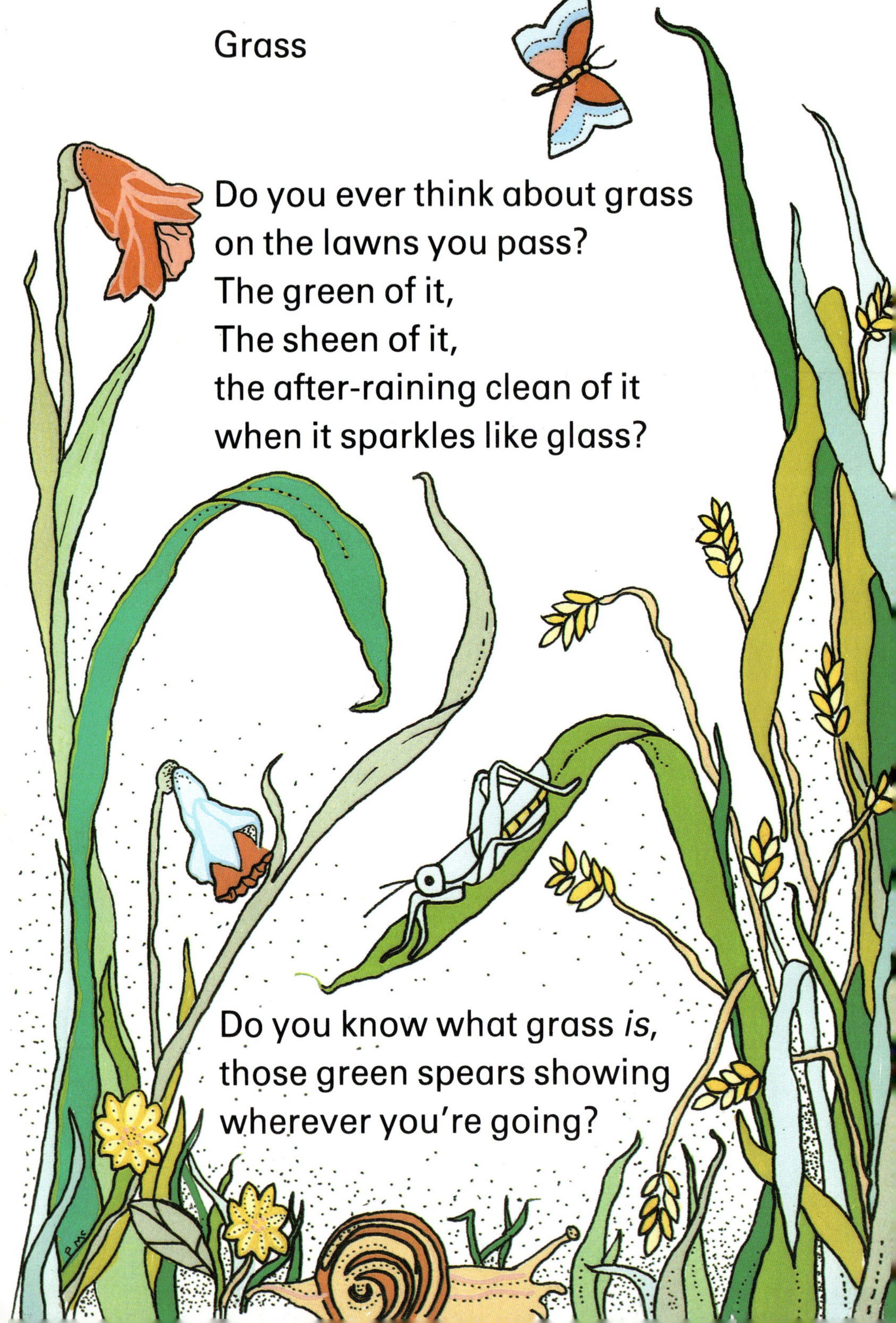

Grass

Do you ever think about grass
on the lawns you pass?
The green of it,
The sheen of it,
the after-raining clean of it
when it sparkles like glass?

Do you know what grass *is*,
those green spears showing
wherever you're going?

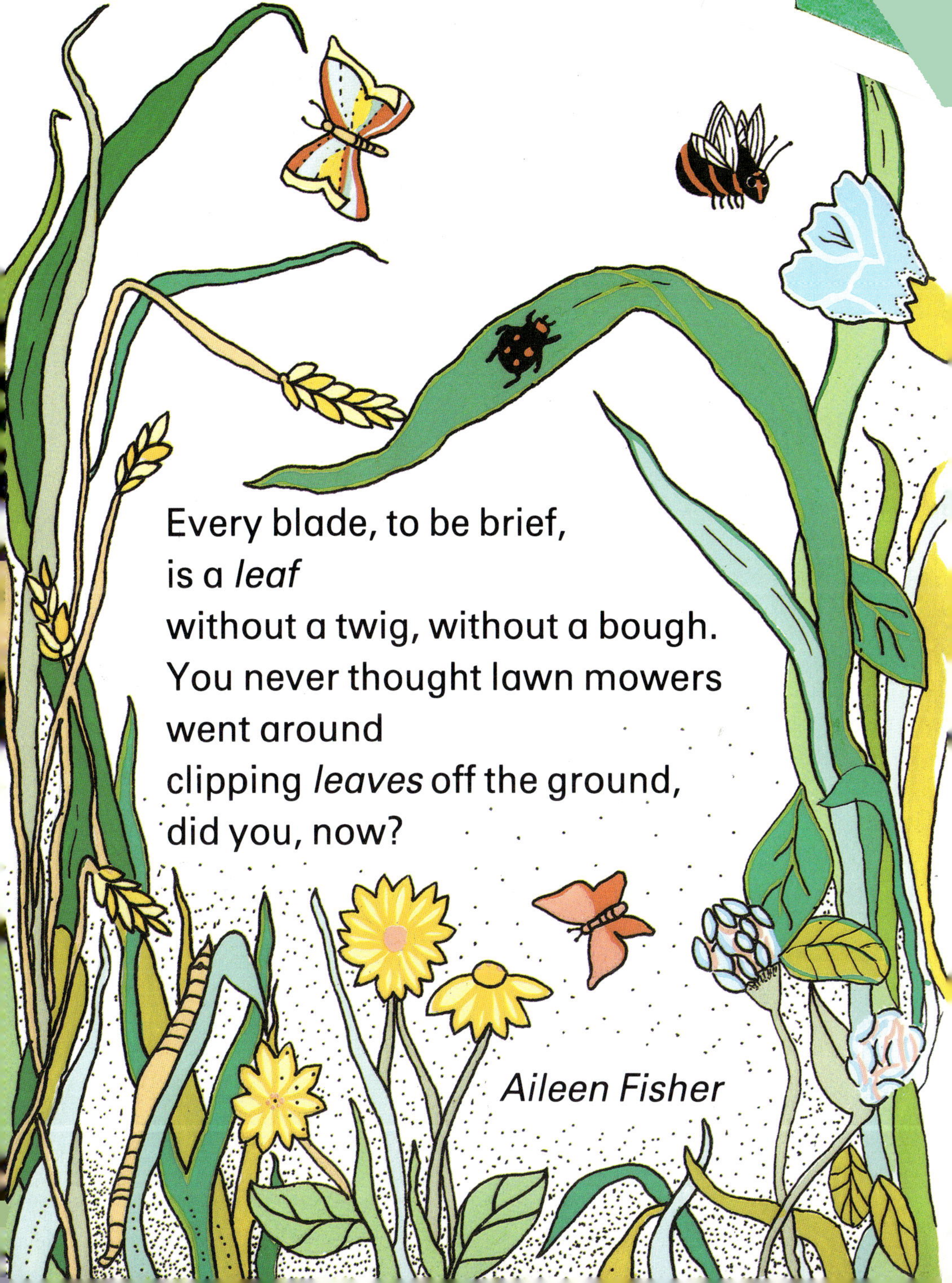

Every blade, to be brief,
is a *leaf*
without a twig, without a bough.
You never thought lawn mowers
went around
clipping *leaves* off the ground,
did you, now?

Aileen Fisher

Peter and the Wolf

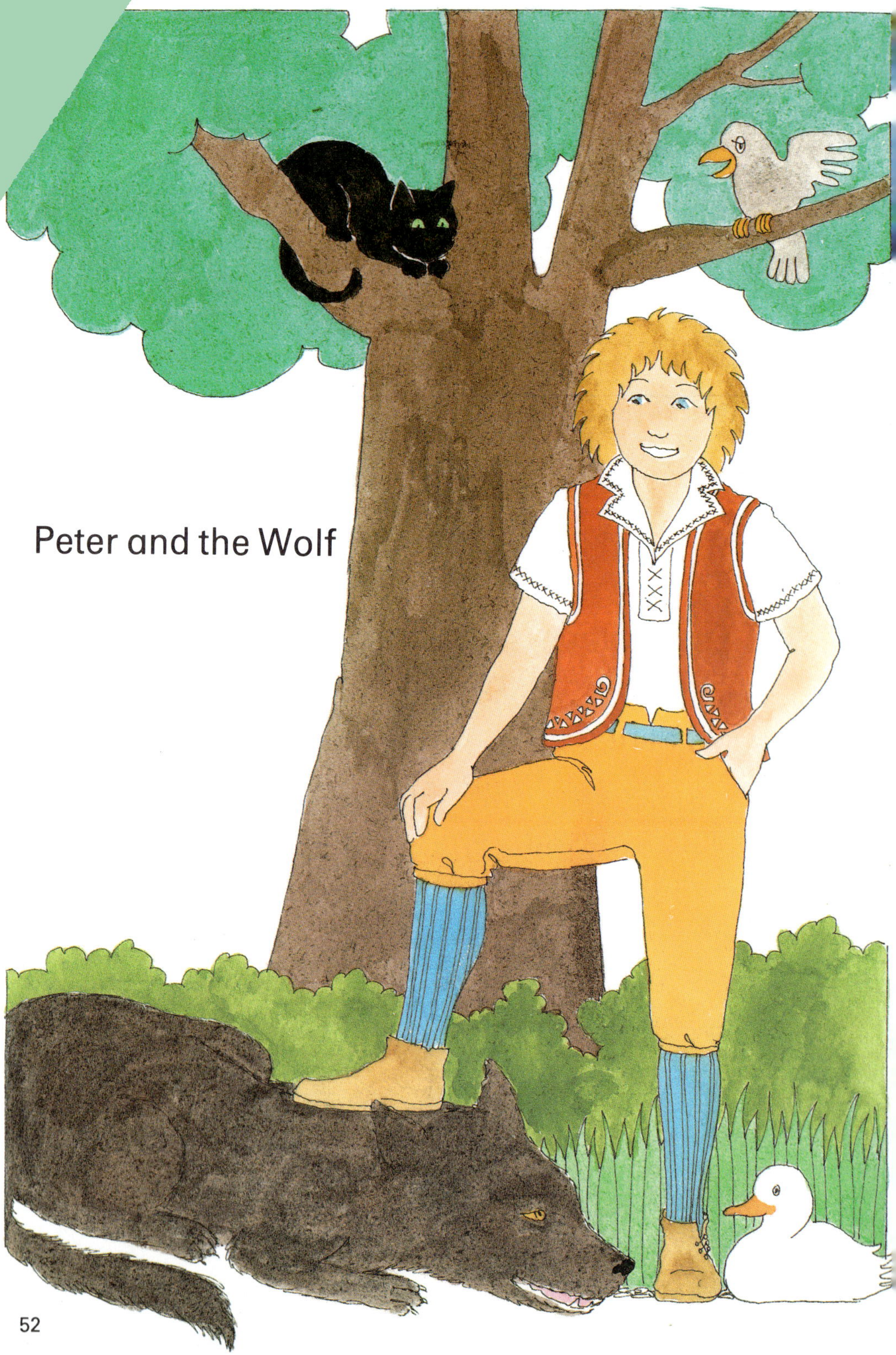

In a faraway place, a boy called Peter went out into his garden one morning. His friend the bird was sitting in a great big tree.

'Good morning, Peter,' sang the little bird.

'Good morning, little bird,' said Peter. 'I am coming out to play with you.'

'Good,' said the little bird.

So Peter opened the gate and went out into the field to see his little friend.

Peter gate

Soon a little duck came walking up to the gate. She was pleased to see that it was open.

'Now I can leave this garden and go and have a swim in the pond,' she said to herself.

When the little bird saw the duck, he flew down to the pond.

'You're a very funny bird,' he said to the duck. 'You cannot fly like me.'

'Who are you to talk?' quacked the duck. 'You cannot swim like me.'

They talked and talked like this, so they did not see that there was something coming across the fields.

swim pond talk quacked

Out of the bushes came a big black cat. When he saw the bird and the duck he said to himself, 'I'll have a lovely dinner today. I'll have that little bird first!'

But Peter saw the cat just in time. 'Look out!' he shouted.

Very quickly, the bird flew away, up into a great big tree and out of the cat's way.

The duck quacked from the pond. 'I am very lucky that cats do not like the water,' she said to herself.

Just then, Peter's Grandfather came out of the house. When he saw Peter outside the gate, he was not very pleased.

'Peter!' he shouted. 'Come back into this garden now! Must I tell you every day not to go into that field? It is too near the woods. Just what would you do if a wolf came out of the woods?'

But Peter was not a bit afraid.

'I am a big boy now, Grandfather,' he said. 'And no wolf could get me!'

'That's what you think!' said Grandfather. And he made Peter come back into the garden.

'Now you stay here!' said Grandfather. 'I am going back inside to have a little sleep.'

Just as soon as Peter was back in his garden, it happened. A great big wolf came running out of the woods!

The cat ran up into the tree when he saw the wolf. The little bird hopped up and down on the branches. And the duck quacked and quacked from the pond.

What a noise they all made!

happened

The little duck was so afraid as she quacked all by herself in the pond. She could see the bird in the tree and she wanted to be with her friend.

So out of the pond she hopped and began to run. But her legs were not very long and she could not run very fast. The wolf came nearer and nearer.

'Run! Run!' shouted the cat and the bird as they hopped up and down in the tree.

But the little duck could not get away. In one big mouthful the wolf gobbled her up!

---

long fast gobbled

'That bad wolf has eaten my friend the duck,' cried the little bird. 'Why did she try to run away?'

The cat looked out from the branches on the tree. And the little bird looked out too as he hopped about the branches. He was trying to stay as far away from the cat as he could.

And under the tree, the wolf walked around and around, looking up at them.

Peter had seen what had happened as he stood in his garden. Into the house he ran and out he came with a long rope. Then he jumped up on the wall and swung himself up into the tree.

'Fly down, now,' Peter called to the little bird as he sat on the strong branch. 'Fly around and around the wolf. But don't let him get you!'

The little bird did just as Peter asked. Around and around the wolf he flew.

The wolf jumped and snapped at the little bird, but the bird was too fast for the wolf. He flew away every time.

---

rope snapped

As the wolf was jumping and snapping at the little bird, he did not see what Peter was doing. So Peter quickly swung his rope and caught the wolf by the tail.

The wolf jumped up and down, this way and that, trying to get away from the rope. But the rope was very strong and Peter had tied one end of it to a branch on the tree.

The more the wolf jumped, the more he was caught by the rope.

---

caught   tail   tied   end

Just then, Peter heard a shout as some men came running out of the woods. They had been looking for the wolf too.

'Look at Peter!' cried one of the men. 'He has caught the wolf all by himself!'

'My friends helped me,' Peter called. 'Now you must help me take him to the zoo.'

zoo

But just then they all heard something. It was a soft quacking noise. And it was coming from inside the wolf!

'My friend the duck!' cried Peter. 'She is still inside the wolf. The wolf gobbled her up in one big mouthful!'

'Pull the wolf up and down with that rope,' called one of the men. 'The wolf will have to open his big mouth and the little duck will fall out.'

And that's just what happened!

pull

'What's all this noise?' cried Grandfather. 'What has happened? I've been trying to sleep!'

'I said I was not afraid, Grandfather,' said Peter. 'I have caught the wolf. Come and help us take him to the zoo.'

So off they all went to the zoo. First came Peter, with the little bird sitting on his hat. And the lucky little duck walked with him.

Next came the men with the wolf. And then along came Grandfather and the cat.

'This is all very well,' Grandfather said to himself. 'But what if Peter had not caught that wolf? What would have happened then?'